The Apricot Tree

and other poems

Books by Elmo Howell:
MISSISSIPPI HOME-PLACES
WINTER VERSES
MISSISSIPPI SCENES
THE APRICOT TREE AND OTHER POEMS

Elmo Howell

"The Apricot Tree

and other poems"

Contents

I. On Finding a Confederate Note

II. Tennessee Williams at the Moon Lake Casino

III. Come Away

IV. Intensive Care

V. The Cherry Trees of Audubon Park

I

On Finding a Confederate Note

The Sallet

I pulled into the drive just to turn around—
I couldn't do less at the house where I was born;
Empty now—though I didn't notice the desolation,
Things were happening so fast.
At the moment of shifting gear
When I stuck my head out the window to see all,
A new green turned in the trees, the light changed,
And a frame fell out of time:—
My mother was coming out of the garden with a
        mess of sallet in her apron
(It was about time for the mail to run)
And I heard my father's hammer below, at the crib
        perhaps,
Above the cluck cluck cluck of the chickenyard;
And every genial god of home was busy with the
        April morning.
But clicked again—
The frame fell back into the inexorable file,
And I was left once more alone.
Poetry, what is it but the indulgence of a moment—
Like pulling into an unused drive—
In the hapless knowledge of one day's passing into
        another.

The Word

When I was a boy listening in,
They never said the word
(Unless awful mad or in a big hurry)
But beat about the bush with it,
Half polite, half silly:
Laws-a-Massy!
And clapped their hands.
But in that tribal holding back,
A feudal leg at the foot of the hill,
Lay gentleness and forbearance—
    what little we had—
One to another,
And every dead-sure thing.
And the different light on Sunday morning.
(Also, they forgot sometimes, but that was
    all right too.)

Home Is So Sad Now

Home is so sad now. Because of the silence.
It could take loss, grief, hope stilled at birth,
Pain the young inflict on the old,
Coffins being borne out—
All that set it off,
Enfolding in its bosom them that came hurt.
It knew how to manage—
A great house, holding up its head among houses.
But no one comes now,
No one quarrels, loves, wounds.
No one takes away the clock that stopped.
The swing moves only in the northwind.
It waits. It asks when I come up in the yard,
What are you going to do with me now?

The White Oak

The white oak stands by the kitchen ell
To announce the seasons and guard the watershelf—
And surely would not run away if it could.
But trees—are they at peace with fixity?
Other things are not.
Though generous of gesture,
Do they resent the creatures—
Darting, looping, soaring in delirious passage?
Or man, who soars too
But comes down at last to build a house,
Settling by a tree to grow old with?—
And they become like one another.
A tree and a good man are happy and do not wish to be
    anywhere else.
They know the horizons and where the weather
    comes from,
They attach certain stars,
And when you come back they are always there.

The Quince Tree

The quince tree stood on a hillside
And my grandmother hoed around it—
Bearing a few mottled fruit in October
Under fuzz pale green.
Not like apples or pears—
Not like anything;
But mine, all mine, ranged in the safe to mellow,
Where we went to look
In the days of proprietary rights.

When the bus stopped in the mountains,
A village woman cried, lifting a basket,
"Membrillos! Membrillos!"
Out of what certitudes long sent packing,
I called out, "What are those! What are those!"
"Membrillos, Señor. Para usted."
And I dropped the magazine,
Hanging in the window a thousand miles from home.
The sun picked up a shawl and a boy's face—
        and wizened eyes found out.
"Membrillos, Señor. Para te. Para te."

What is love but choosing—
Turning all the others out—
And saying to quinces in the cool dark safe,
        Get ripe!

Little Boy

The July morning laughed and leapt—
The little branch a window kept;
Floors creaked—hushed—afraid;
Grandsires waited in the shade.

Legs so round and full of fun,
His father fixed his hopes upon
Lay still and yellow on the cloth—
And on his mouth a snowy froth.

All night long beside the bed
His mother held her nestling's head—
Till in the door an angel stood
To cut for God so firm a bud.

His brother, a limber boy,
Felt no selfish rival's joy
In expectations orthodox
And wept beside the little box.

Not Many Could Have Known Her

When the procession turned into the highway,
The cars we met, according to custom, pulled
    off to one side—
Some even into the ditch—
And waited.
Not many could have known her, surely only a few,
And some would have liked to go on.
But we went slow on her day
And took the salute in a dignified way.
As she would have done,
Exact and formal in such matters—
Counting obeisances no doubt if she could.
On her way to church in a pretty new dress.

The New Car

On a winter morning, daring the whole world,
My father drove our new car by the schoolhouse.

They said I was sick—-but could have gone to school
Except for the car, and felt guilty and was afraid,

But on the backseat tried to be happy.
My father bent over the wheel, my mother wore
    a blue hat—

And we were riding, riding in the strange morning
While other people worked and went to school.

Where, where do the mornings go?
When I think of the tracks on the furrowed hillside—
My brave father, my mother's face—

I ask in wonder that the least should perish.
Where are the shouts by the schoolhouse?

The Leash

The day I got lost at the fair—
    Cut off from the hand of home—
The fat lady liked little boys,
    The man on the wall said Come.

Wild horses—and a monster-mirth—
    Sent me reeling back.
East and west were gone for good
    And time began to tick;

When a hand reached out from the crowd—
    A wild and angry face
Lined and locked in tribal doom—
    And pulled me in to peace.

The merry-go-round went round,
    Banners bloomed afresh
For all sweet creatures foreordained
    A sure and certain leash.

Hearing Once
The Whippoorwill

Hearing once the whippoorwill in a great city,
I awoke to vexation—for how could that be?—
Not knowing that I lay again in my father's
    empty house
Beside his woods and orchard.
Gray light staggered in on the May morning,
And I stood by the window—
As I had done so many times before,
When there was pasture and tillage and men
    calling to mules—
With two voices in the kitchen conterminous
    with breath,
Or so I thought—
Though fudged in their commission.
How is it that the past cannot be summoned
But comes when it will, unsought,
Standing by a window on the edge of action?

The voices went under just before the call to
    breakfast,
Turned in to silence with the bird.

On Finding A Confederate Note

Was that part of the legacy too?
In a fruit jar, sealed, with a few black Mexican coins
At the bottom of a closet.
Who put it there,
With what care—or disregard,
Not knowing where or why?—
And the old deserted house moved into a wider landscape
To contain all ultimates of defeat and being left alone,
Discounted on a broken field.
"Issued at the Capital, February 17, 1864..."
From the pledge of a nation to nothing on God's earth—
Through disbelief, despair, grief
To blank accord, and innocency of all knowledge—
Something could be made of that!
But on that afternoon, held to the light of
     a kitchen window,
The note flared and trembled with life, crowing of empire—
Caisson, smoke, pennon and white mounts,
And the desolation of houses.
Humoring the moment, deaf to dead walls about me,
I heard again the rattling drive
And the rider, arms outspread:
The dead, the dead have died again!
It is not a matter of flags and lost fields
Nor battlements above the gate:
The lares are taken!
Children booted away,
The old—and old of heart—
Consigned to a land of tombs—and the new faces.
That morning in '65, when the word came
     down from Richmond.

The Death Of An Old Man

Relinquishment of heat
  Long after joy fell
Left only eyes
  To brave the mineral.

Consequence of vinegar
  Lay fierce about the bone;
Moulting of bark and burr,
  Residue of sun.

II

Tennessee Williams at the Moon Lake Casino

Tennessee Williams
At The Moon Lake Casino

After services at the Church of the Epiphany in Tunica,
Tom and his grandfather pulled round by the lake for lunch.
It was a glorious day in the parking lot, made manifest
        in birdcall and something hanging in a bush.
In the dining room—an expanse of white and the
        landlady's flower garden ranged round a water—
The gentlemen were honored with a table at the window,
The landlady herself presiding
In a complexity of menials, coffee, and tiny tiny biscuits
        that melt in your mouth.
She'd been to church herself—starch in your bonnet
        on a day like this—
And what a fine young man the Reverend had there
        with him!
For whom, in the quiet upstairs, mystery held on—
Down what dark corridor
And at what cracked door in night's configuration?
Back home in the rectory, Tom slept upstairs
And looked out on stained glass windows—
Across an alley where mean boys lurked.
In the complacency of flesh,
And benediction of white linen and the bright canna bed,
He arose and thanked his grandfather for his chicken—
At fourteen or fifteen, was it?—
Well pleased with irony
And Mrs. Stilicho's Sunday dinner at the
        Moon Lake Casino.

Two Young Boys On The Way To The Pool

Pausing on the trestle to give full measure,
Horsing around,
Blue and Green take on enterprise:—
Hiatus in the sun!
With a shout,
        shimmer,
                and pearls all over the place.

Great city of Nineveh!
O ye uncircumcised on the railroad track,
Perilously on the edge!
Any day now the Missioners will come
To consult with Head Men, with spears,
And line up ye louts for Mass and a good feed.
In the sadness of summer, waiting,
Stripped down
For the Holy Ghost to come upon you
    in the locker room,
Southern Station, YMCA.

Sunday Afternoon In The Quarter

After High Mass,
Pigeons and painters alight in the Square
And breakfast loafers at the Coffee Pot talk in
    low voices, looking out the window.
Around two or two-thirty,
The day begins with a scattering of bar stools at
    Tony Bacino's
And Mozart in the courtyard where they had the
    fight last night.
The long afternoon looks up with every shape in
    the door—
But turns in on itself, puts moral questions and
    lights a cigarette.
On the levee, promenaders check whose ship has
    come in;
While below, two nuns join the crowd at the
    fountain to see a fellow ducked—
Who has a great deal to say for himself!
The crowd disperse to have a likeness drawn.
Bourbon comes to around four,
Where just inside the door a black girl bangs
PLEASE DO TO ME WHAT YOU DONE TO MARIE
ON BACK STREET SATURDAY NIGHT—
Shows her teeth and takes you in.
Streets converge in heat and rapidity of nerves—
Till dry fronds stir and the cloud above Rampart
    looks mean.
Down Ursulines—past dependencies where slave girls
    told their beads—
                                                    Dark

Dark faces hold to stoop, while banana leaves
        lash the new light
And window curtains advertise shelter.
In the vortex over the city,
An abeyance of will (as in the stillness of God)
For an assessment of flesh, stained ceiling—
Or of nothing at all.
After the storm,
To Market, to Market (where all forgather)
To drink brown coffee
And be transcendental—by golden gutters
Swept clean
Of festering fruit, banana peel and where
        a horse has stood.

The Hen's Nest

*In his early youth the Emperor Honorius made some progress in
the exercises of riding and drawing the bow, but soon relinquished
these fatiguing occupations for the amusement of feeding poultry;
which became the serious and daily care of the monarch of the West.*
—Gibbon

Little yellow fleece-balls
Toddling to wing—
With one peek back!
O sweet security of straw and
    warm feathers
In a rude box nailed to the
    wall.
This world! This world!
While Alaric makes ready.

The Big Wash

Every night the world goes under
And out of the big wash turns up man—
Sitting on the edge of the bed, looking
    forlornly out the window.
Out there, a bird sits on a wire and looks back,
He's been under too.
Things happen in a wallow,
Something—ever so little—
In the way we come out and shake off—
Reach for a smoke, tie a shoe, check the weather—
The old drag and drain
And now recurrent question:
How long can this keep up?—
Just for a twinkle,
Before coffee
    and the wings of morning.
The bird just sits there, stupid thing—
Squats one time
And sits on.

The Last Smoker

The old man sat in the smoking car
On the last train out
On the last day.
The media were there, a few public officials,
But mostly the curious, in the offhand pull
        towards a crowd,
Even at that late hour.
One delegation was organized, with banners—
And restrained satisfaction on hard-bitten faces;
For, as their leader kept repeating through a
        megaphone,
They had come a long way.
But the crowd, indifferent, kept to the window,
Pointing at, some cheering, the old man
About to take off for a ride into history.
He sat all alone in the vast car with a book
        in his lap,
Eyes straight ahead, profoundly abstract.
In the blue oblation of dead air
He looked like an idol taking in time,
Adept, profane.
They didn't know what to make of him.

Grasmere Turn

Above Dove Cottage, along the road to Ambleside,
Green shoots of violet, cow parsley,
And here and there the lesser celandine.
One night in March, William had a toothache—
The wind was in the treetops and rain came into
        his room—
But went in the morning to compose at the sheepfold.
Dorothy sauntered in the garden while Molly
        weeded turnips,
Then came inside to read King John and make a shoe.
But it was no good at the sheepfold.
Strained with much altering, William returned sadly tired
        (with threatenings of the piles)
And lay till past 5.
In the afternoon
Dorothy sate in the orchard, stuck peas, and walked to
        Rydale wood—past the lowing of cattle—
To gather sods and plants for Dove.
To be set out by moonlight.

How I should have liked to go too, gathering sods while
        William slept—
Not knowing cow parsley or the lesser celandine of course,
But could have dug and carried the basket
(Over the stepping stones on the way home!)
And been foolish and happy.

On Seeing HRH The Prince Of Wales Watercolours In Memphis

They seemed small, scores of them, in a rather tame
    arrangement,
With a video going in the background:
Sandringham, Windsor, Balmoral, the Castle of Mey—
Resounding names
With muted pageantry lying just beneath the Prince's
    wry comment.
This, I decided, was the plus and ranged round the
    room two or three times.
But later—on city streets and through a piece of
    March woods—
Is it possible, I asked myself, that in such a grand
    state with the gods
Loneliness is written on the morning sky?
Caithness, A Side of Lochnagar, "The Elegant Chance
    of that Single Cypress," Down the Dee Valley
    Towards Balmoral Without Rain—
All the paintables—are they set there to hurt one?
Just like the rest of us
(In a scaled-down show of course),
Turning towards home on a rainy afternoon.

III

Come Away

A Bluebird Is Like Love

It came in the morning, silent in the apple tree—
And vanished like that.
For this is no longer bluebird country.
I knew it would go away—accustomed to exception—
But come again,
Turning up sudden, when no one thought,
In the orchard or precincts of knothole by the
        pasture fence.
Renewing the heart,
Saying no to drought.

A bluebird is like love,
A silent enduring presence, here or just there,
Aloof, not squandered in the waste places,
But waiting the moment
Unheeded—
Gathering, gathering to light on the mailbox
And turn the foolish day to splendor.

Come Away

Will you come away with me again?
Won't you come?
Leave the ragged race unrun
For the little boat at two and carelessness
    of sun
On a cove where dreams put out to sea?
Oh, what is this life but stolen blue!
I hope you think so too.

It's not the same if you don't go.
I am but half myself I know.
The sun is not a jolly guy
And others' pleasures do but hurt the eye
When evening waits by a lonely motel room.
I hope you come.

The Deputy Tree

Within my garden pale,
Poor captives from far fields and headlands
Bloom in villein state—
In new seasons and in line with their master's
    emotion.
How useful they are to keep secrets,
Bearing in true faces
What cannot be said or perhaps even thought again—
Old loves and losses,
The fierce impress of passion spent—
Or velleity of a morning.
They help the years to go gently,
Then are gathered one day for a party.
But do they—do flowers have a life of their own
With the bee and the wind to give their grace
    to the sun?
Man pokes about with his hoe and crippled heart
And says what's what.
Flowers grow fat and are happy, I think, but not on
    their own terms.
This viburnum, for example, in sweet syllabub white
(Sometimes I come out at night to watch it glow)—
You stood here one afternoon in shirtsleeves, an arm
    along the bough,
And stole its essence.
Now it is only a deputy tree—
In service, with an appointed time, summoned by a bell.
A garden is an arrangement precarious as life,
An old servitude
Much too involved to think about.

At The Seaside

The ship diminished on a far blue line;
You stood at the ripple looking out—
Perfectly still in the sun's granting.

To the west, a motel and moments of earth;
And below the sea oats at the tide's last stand,
An old couple, dug in, ignored us,

Hooded like crabs. With too much awareness
You played the margin in black trunks;
The old, surveying their ship and all that was lost,

Held to binoculars, seeing, not seeing, seeing.
Does happiness go to visit—seek out with round arms—
The ones it can humble when it comes to show itself?

(But stalwart suns go in, accede to dark—
The gulls tell all. In nearness to joy
I think on loneliness and death.)

Later, much later, we sat on the balcony
Withdrawn in quietness—watching with the old
Where a child pushed back the defeated sea.

Sometimes I Think That
I Should Like To Be A Stone

Sometimes I think that I should like to be a stone
Absolved from heat and the necessity of joy.
How willingly the winds should have their way,
    buffeting like little children,
And the vivid soft creatures in transit about me:
The field mouse crying for help,
A butterfly,
A daisy nestling close,
The shepherd with his pipe—
All unfortunates on journey
Who wanton awhile and weep at evening.
But I should not listen nor concern myself.
A stone has no odyssey—
And shall I say no heart.
It takes its cue from stars
Fixed beyond delight and the catch of breath.

Look How The Light Falls

If only we could break away for a little while!
It must be fine where the white shelf waits
And at nine o'clock clouds come up by the
    island—
Disengage the old self, so sure,
For a generous latitude and a new sun's daft
    horizon.
Look how the light falls there by the boathouse
    and a palm leans out.
Standing on the boardwalk before the call to
    dinner,
We disengage
And look at the other side of the question.
By the sea there is always celebration.

Shall we go, shall we consider—
Spell the mule at the end of the row,
To think on these things in the security
    of rut?
Or is it too late now—
Even to remember
The sea's wash and an open window
Where strange flowers bloomed in the night?
Hills reach out to a different star—
And we have taken their savor,
Stood up by the weatherboarded church so long
In the staunchness of seasons.

A Gay Tripper

A gay tripper drunk on sun
Fell into my hands one day to show
Close-up what vagrant beauties be.
But in that vile parleying
Brushed a wing—
A weft designed for gold,
Now sodden mould.
I held my breath in shame—and let it go
Marked in folly evermore.
Innocent of jest,
The poor dumb beast
Rose in morning joy aloft,
Bearing blind grief
Midst irony of leaf and garden croft—
And took an incubus to sea
To hang upon the mating tree.

The Guest

(after Primo Levi)

Since it has grown late,
I will accept your hospitality,
But only a light fare, if you will,
And a bed to sleep in alone.
I like a bare floor and lamp oil
And a hearth that dies out in the night
    on old frames harboring lost skies.
But most of all to be in an honest man's
    house.
And in the morning, I shall give you my
    poems,
Slender like these,
To be read by only a few
But pleasant to hold in the hand.
And then we shall part, my friend, each
    to his own cares,
Since, as I said, it has grown late.

IV

Intensive Care

Estuary

The poem is famous—everybody knows it—
But too simple to understand,
Or so I had been told;
Though puzzling when you come to look at the words.
I had not really read it till I heard it once
    over a coffin.
Then the meaning gathered—
Beyond words, which get in the way—
In the race of an old man's heart crossing an estuary
    at sunset with his nurse.
I saw what he meant—though not in the words,
But in something that rushed round, through and over
    them,
Drowning—
Till I was blind with tears.
I did not know that he was such a great poet.

When I Saw The Gentle Nun

When I saw the gentle nun in the line at Krogers
Standing behind the woman whose baby had puked
     on her shoulder,
With another between her legs—
Plus an old crab up at the register—
I said to myself,
What would we do,
How could any moment be endured without
     a symbol?
That full, perfect and sufficient sacrifice
And still expanse of supernumerary white
Stood between me and the soilure of this world—
Late one afternoon
At Krogers quick checkout,
When I was in a hurry.

Intensive Care

Once as I watched an old man die
Who hadn't nearly enough of sky,
I couldn't help wondering why
He was buckled down the way he was,
With tubular cords of every size
In and out and over his eyes—
Eyes pleading with me to get him loose.
The doctor came in and all the house
Stood up in white, still as a mouse.
He found all vital signs alert,
Checked a dial, watched the bubbles spurt
And wrote it down on his chart.
But never touched him where it hurt.
Then they moved on down to Number Four,
And the clock on the wall said one minute more—
For this was strictly Intensive Care.

Fleabane

Patchy on the hill and in the fields
But strong along creekside,
Like blackberry drift in May,
Little flower—here in the palm of my hand—
You promise what no one wants any more
And gather into symbol in the late October sun
A voluptuary sadness.

One time you mattered—
When dogs, tail-knocking, slept in the house;
When boys said Sir, and tall corn grew in the
    New Ground
And signs in the Book of Revelation.

Autumn Colors

This new sky is a mockery of blue.
Better to look back
To April and the cracked robin shell under
    the hedge—
When the course was not known or thought about
Nor where one slept at night.
Ah, sweet deployment of earth, two by two,
    outside the sheltering rock.
Now the homeless gather round, insistent, whining,
Mocked by blue and early chill
And the withdrawal of God's favor.
Their time has run out, the time to consider and
    build houses.
Grasshoppers sortie on the hillside—
Where a gay party assemble to observe death.
They point, amble, throw out their arms—
    and settle againsst the bus
To lift a glass across the valley,
    so lovely,
Beyond the crofted wheatfields and the churchyard
Where summer lies slain.

The Flowers Of Late November

How can it be that grace is still with us?
In a disheveled bed, blue velvet appears,
And on Thanksgiving afternoon, I left my rake
      for a yellow butterfly
Dipping in out of the southwest
Where a flashlight sun pointed the way.
I stood a moment caught up in the mystery,
Peripheral under my pine tree.
Tempting providence, I said,
As the light went down in the ruined garden,
Unless their knowledge is greater than mine;
And turned away towards evening
In a dear solicitude
(Which I could no longer call pain)
For all fond creatures thoughtlessly entreating
      the purple and gold—
And for all unfinished tasks.

November Pears

November pears lie spotted on the ground,
Glut of a very good year.
Squirrels come in from the fog to check the
    bee-fest
And to sample one maybe—plenty for all.
On a fallow hillside, the ancient tree outdid
    itself this year
And shaking loose of summer, doesn't even
    notice
Two leprous waifs on the edge of the world
    coming with buckets.
Though backporch, cellar and windowsill are
    full,
Rejoicing in plenty—too much goodness—
Surely something can be done with a few more.
A few more for what's up ahead—
And to fill in a morning that stood empty-handed
Till we thought of the pears.

The Snow

When the snow came
A new grace fell across the city
Chairs were pushed back, scissors and thread
    returned to the basket,
For the window was a wonder—a squirrel jumped
    to the sill—
With people turning out in old gear,
Laughing,
Heads up against the north!
It was strange to see so many happy people
Speaking to everybody, just everybody,
Smiling their manners—
But hurried, rushing on to something.
That was the marvel of snow,
A world patched up to sudden trust
And energy of heart,
As if the Fall had not happened.
But waning at sundown,
Poor starved ghosts,
With lights, the building of fires,
And settling down to one still thought:—
Innocence came back for a little while—
And we didn't know what to do.
On a day so like all the others
Until that dark afflatus in the west.

The Young Beeches

In late winter
When most trees have turned in for the night,
Young beeches, in full dress, appear in the woods,
Now open for inspection,
Like careless brown unbrellas spread on the floor.
Copse-orphans,
Where do they come from?
Whoever sees a beech tree today,
Globular, honey-masted for pigs,
Claiming a wide circumference?
(I remember just one
Whose antique roots peeped out on white sand.
We went to the spring with buckets
And waited by the black pot, the bench and
        battling stick—
To be told.)
In woods vestigial
The orphans assemble, lovely in desolation,
Giving new interest before whippoorwills;
Before ditch-willows stake out new green
And the hills give in to summer.

The Lost Children

Dear and so sad
The plaint of waking birds before morning light.
At my bedside window, I peer into the dark
    of another day,
And the voices bring back what day has no time for:—
Departed half-joys,
Innocent vanities long since forborne,
Beauty unmerited—and hope that hurts to remember;
Profferings of bliss, startling like flowers,
    fading, untaken;
Ingratitude—and the wound on a vanished face.
These are the ghosts of earth-shift,
The vapors of morning
When time takes over and the small birds are tremulous.
I think that they are the souls of little lost children
Come back to play in the front yard again
Before they were called away.

How Did They The Nameless Dead

How did they the nameless dead—
Row after row, undefined by stone or bone,
But quick once, with a thing in hand
Like you and me!—
How did they do on the day the word went out?
After the sally of the sick room,
With hope rebounding like a lark, almost at song,
Till earth cut in
And light was not light but a glazed window?
(Was it always the same?)
How did they do?
How did they handle the faces drawing in,
The aproned hands,
The silence,
The birds in the eaves?
Anyhow—they managed, they came;
Threw something over their shoulders for the
        long queue across the hills
And kept the appointed hour.
So many of them.

The Invitation

(after T'ao Ch'ien)

This morning I heard a knock at my door—
My neighbor, who came in smiles and I could see
    with good news.
They were giving a party—how nice if I could come
    too.
It is not fair, he said, to shut yourself off
    from the company of so many good people.
We hope to greet you at our door at seven.
I thank you, my friend, I said.
And I am truly sorry.
But the time has passed—the tree has bent to the wind—
Or perhaps it was only my nature that kept me
    out of tune.
But come, sit down please, and let us talk awhile.
It is a lovely day for friends to meet,
And my odd ways are of no moment to anyone.

(for B. J.)

V

The Cherry Trees
of
Audubon Park

Haggard Day Lay In The Window

When I entered the room
Haggard day lay in the window—
Beside a gray stone, a lovely O,
Washed round a summer sea where I purloined it—
A piece of time brought home in my suitcase.
Though it never seemed right there.
I stood in the void of light and held it in my
     hand a long time.
Looking out—
But nothing, nothing.
Rejecting, like a cold heart,
The spurious little sun proffering heat.
Not knowing how to feel, on a difficult morning,
Or what the manners were,
I laid it back in the accustomed place.

The Respite

What is pain but a nudge of death!
　　In fair light where all is well
　　A dark secret knell
Puts a term on breath.

Night shuts in alone.
　　Four walls close
　　On what must be. The clutched pillow knows
Ultimates of bone.

O sweet remission! When it comes,
　　The poor head sinks in peace.
　　The sudden stars ring out release!
And morning, how it hums!

Miss Soonie

Miss Soonie has lived at the Nursing Home ever so long,
And at Christmas my neighbor and I go by to see her.
This year, we saw right off that she has a new roommate.
"How have you been, Miss Soonie?"—sitting on the edge
     of the bed with a little lipstick on.
"She's been crazy!" the roommate said.
We laughed, laughed it off—Miss Soonie laughed too
And dug into the little presents we brought her.
The house was hot. Family pictures lined her corner
And she began to tell about them, pointing—
Ending every story with a reckoning: "All deceased"—
Even fresh young faces—even children.
"Deceased! Deceased!" the old woman cried.
     "Deceased yourself!"
The mailwoman came by with a pleasant black face and
     stood in the door.
"Hit the jackpot today, Soonie," and dropped a red
     Christmas card in her lap.
"These are my friends," Miss Soonie said, rising to the
     occasion. "I want you to meet..."
"Hi!" the mailwoman said and went on down the hall.
"They are good Christian people," Miss Soonie said—
Little edges of the nerves trembling for gentleness,
"The Lord has been good to me."
We decided to stop off on the way out to see where Miss
     Soonie goes to church. She told us about it.
The hall was banked with flowers.
We met three wheelchairs and had to work our way through.
"Hi, Buster!" one of them said. The others laughed.
                                                      Later

Later at McDonalds it was Christmassy there too.
The waiters were upbeat and got right to us—
    and we found a corner to ourselves.
More and more came in, calling out to their friends,
    till the place was full—
But the music was good, the young people were happy—
    they were playing all Christmas songs—
And we decided to forget the whole thing for another year.

The Red Handkerchief

In the house where I was born,
I stood in the hall one day and watched
    a coffin being carried out.
An old man with a red handkerchief in his hand
    ran after it—
His face was torn—
But they caught him at the edge.

The Cedar Bough

On the day before Christmas, I walked in
    the deep woods
And brought back a small bough of cedar.
It was something I could do—
And it lies on a shelf beside my books,
    ungarlanded,
Full of health.
Cold has no mettle against dark green,
No wound.
I like that.
Cedar is straightforward, just right,
Speaking in the night of clean places
Far from the roadside,
And of some strength that I do not understand
But believe in and will wait for.
There can be no harm in that.

Jonah

Fish me out, O Lord!
Batten my heart on Thy green verge,
And I'll be bait for Thee.
Shed my shame,
And I will go to that great city and at
    the gates tell all!
It could not be but was!—
Under the gourd vine laughing.
Fish me, God!
Just show me a sky and new sands burning!

Grief Cannot Long Impale A Garden

My feet knowing, in the maimed morning,
    led into a garden.
The rose was not really strutting herself,
Birds were not crowing,
And the sweet sap was sorry for its business.
Yes, I said, I can sit here awhile in a well-ordered
    place.
The bee had not heard—
Off on a run—
And I got in his way.
But the plants were anxious, waiting around me,
Every grassblade was willing to listen—
Which put me to shame.
For I did not come to complain or bring shadow,
I did not want to offend the sun;
And since there was work to be done—
Where others have laid a hand before me—
Went for my hoe.
Grief cannot long impale a garden.
The feet know the way.

Levin in the Oat Field

When Levin went out one morning to mow with
    the peasants,
Leaving his fine brother to sleep till noon,
He knew what he wanted—
He wanted Revolution!
And put his brain into the handle of a scythe.
Mishka was a pretty lad, just married,
And Levin went at it between him and the old man.
They laughed a little at first, he was so clumsy—
But it's all a matter of unbroken swing—
The scythe cut of itself—
Wearing away the world with a drop of sweat.
Beyond the rows of new-cut hay
And the meadow where they found the quail's nest,
The manor house dozed in peace.
At the end of a row they cleaned scythes and drank
    from the stream;
And with children bobbing through the grain with
    bread and beer,
The mowers gathered in a willow run and waited.
"Come, Master, taste our sop," the old man said,
And turned towards the east to pray.
Levin was drunk.
He was not a good mower but did what he was told—
Caught up in the new muscle-rhythm
And a trust he couldn't account for.
In the afternoon they cut the whole of the big meadow
And, with a nip to the lads, moved on to Mashkin Upland
    and wound that up after sundown.
The peasants followed their Master and looked after him.
He made them happy too.

The Apricot Tree

While everyone else was still sleeping,
Oleg got up and made his bed—
Folding the four corners of his blanket to the center
　　as required by regulations—
And tiptoed out of the Cancer Ward.
He stopped on the porch, stood still, and looked out at
　　the world.
It was early spring, with something in the sky and trees that
　　touches even the old and sick—
The first day of Creation, he thought. My morning.
Come live, live! it seemed to say.
His face radiated happiness. Would the apricot tree be in bloom?
It might.
Even the trolley was a new freedom.
Across the bridge, the weak-limbed willows bent into the water,
　　trusting in nature.
An old Uzbec boarded, folded the tram ticket and stuck
　　it in his ear—
A pink touch that made the day seem gayer.
But no apricot tree.
The tearoom was on a balcony that looked down on houses
　　and gardens;
And, to be exotic on this strange morning,
He ordered *kok*, green tea—
A mistake—it had no strength and didn't taste like tea at all.
But he didn't complain, and didn't order anything to eat,
　　though hungry—
Just sat in the sun marveling,

　　　　　　　　　　　　　　　　　　Adopting

Adopting the changeless, unhurried manner of the people
about him.
Then—adjusting his chair into a new position—
He saw from the balcony above the walled courtyard something
pale and transparent.
A weightless rosy balloon?
Or was it a great puff dandelion—
Or an apricot tree!
He sat very still, as if it would go away.
This was the reward for not hurrying. The lesson was—never rush
on without looking around first.
He walked to the railing and looked down on the pink wonder,
His present to himself!
The tree was in a yard enclosed by clay walls, open only to the
sky, and people seemed to live there.
It was like a fire tree, decorated with pink candles on the point
of opening.
But inside pure white,
A tender evolving joy.
Oleg wanted to absorb it all into his eyes and remember it for
a long time.
He wanted to tell the Kadmins about it.
He knew there'd be a miracle.

Now I Adore My Life

Now I adore my life.
The sun in the morning, his appointment with
    the hill,
Eaglet and snail,
And a cloud coming in from the west.
There is so much more to see now and understand,
More engagement with nerves.
The tree trunk is mystery hidden in a crevice,
The stump where honeysuckle gathers has something
    going over my head,
A rose startles and deceives—
But in time I shall know more.
In these headlong days—
I cannot believe it about myself—
Crossing the yard on a mission of mercy,
So many things cry out, waving their arms,
Please, please!—
I quite forget my way.

I adore my life
But cannot pretend it is the same.
Adoration is a parley, beyond embrace.
It is in a sense as if I were dead, looking back;
Or watching perhaps a squirrel in a wire cage—
Pulling up a chair for a demonstration, which is
    reenactment.
Yes, oh yes, I see! I understand
The mock leap and half-rapture—
The made-up day—and horrid flick of knowing

                           In

In the last sun before a hooded cage is
    taken away.
O poor tamed one,
Gone are thy deep woods,
Gone is thy life!
Where knowing was unknowing
In the limb's arch and bounce of sky.

I Think That I Could Live In A Great City

I think that I could live in a great city—
With people and the monumental mortar;
For earth will out;
Some little green thing will say Hi! again.
I should miss my backyard of course:
The dove on a winter morning,
Whippoorwill,
And summer nights that come into the room—
How I should miss them!
But mystery is everywhere, even in the city—
If only in a blade of grass, in a crevice of pavement
    on the way to work;
And I should stop off,
Eddy the herd around me,
And gather into my consciousness for days and
    nights to come,
Checking each morning as I pass.
For I have much in common with a blade of grass.
We live by sufferance—
We look out for weather
And rejoice when the slow rain comes.

I think that I could live in a great city;
Feet will pass, the hard core quicken.
I do not need much green—
Not April, a field of corn, nor where the
    spring runs down—
One blade of grass will do.
And in the wry days, my friend will say, Come!
It's not as bad as all that.
We're right here together, and all will be well.

The Gift

(after Milosz)

A day so happy.
This morning I arose with a good heart and
    went into the garden.
My step had a spring to it.
The sun came up comradely, warming to my hoe
And to the mockingbird's song high on the lightpole.
He has a nest hidden from me, that's what he is saying.
I dug and dug—how the good sweat swung!—
Straightening up to the pleasant ache
(Look at the bee there—he's digging too!)
And to feel the world settling into compass.
Sometimes harmony falls into a train,
For I found myself humming when I came back into
    the house—
Doffing my shoes at my desk.
I don't know why I am happy.
It was a gift for this day.

The Cherry Trees
of Audubon Park

I don't hold much to miracles,
Not as a rule—
Allowing for survival here and there
And a few stupendous moments, unexpected
	and certainly undeserved—
But if you go to Audubon Park at the
	right time—
In morning mist, towards evening, or just
	before a storm—
The cherry trees rise up to greet you
And turn on the whole country!
Visibly breathing, pulsing in a sweet levitation—
About to break free!
No wonder cars slow down.
Just for a day or so in March—
Sometimes early March,
Well ahead of Easter.

Designed and Produced by
Roscoe R. Langford
Langford & Associates
3307 Park Avenue
Memphis, Tennessee 38111